THE STUBBORN PARTICULARS OF GRACE

BOOKS BY BRONWEN WALLACE

The Stubborn Particulars of Grace

Bronwen Wallace

M&S

The Canadian Publishers
McClelland and Stewart
481 University Avenue
Toronto, Ontario M5G 2E9

Canadian Cataloguing in Publication Data
Wallace, Bronwen
The stubborn particulars of grace

Poems.
I S B N 0-7710-8790- X

I. Title.

P S8595. A565 S78 1987   C811'.54   C87-094323- 5
P R9199.3. W355 S78 1987

The publisher makes grateful acknowledgment to the
Canada Council and the Ontario Arts Council for their
financial assistance.

Printed and bound in Canada

Set in Garamond by The Typeworks, Vancouver

for
Cathy Jamieson, Joanne McAlpine,
and Chris Whynot

"Possibility and limitation mean about the same thing."
— Flannery O'Connor

CONTENTS

NEARER TO PRAYERS THAN STORIES

APPEAL

That family joke every Sunday,
all of us for dinner at Grandma's
and my dad asked to give thanks
always mumbling into his plate
and my grandmother always looking up
to say "I didn't hear half of that,"
and my dad always replying "Well, Mother,
I wasn't just talking to you."
The laugh that followed
so predictable, so necessary
that the whole thing sang in my mind,
joined the steaming bowls and platters
moving hand to hand above my head
with the slow, clean words
my aunts and uncles used
to make an anecdote or a bit of gossip
into the story of their lives, that world
I found mysterious as their names became
when I looked at their faces or their arms.

When I look at my mother
on a night in 1953, or maybe '55,
sitting on the lawn at the cottage
with my dad and Frank and Helen, the Americans
from across the lake, who've come over
with a bottle of gin and some Marlboros,
which my father is enjoying, though my mother,
her posture what Protestantism becomes
when the protest's gone, sits prim and uncomfortable.
I'm inside, trying to sleep,
but you can tell it's too hot by how the sheet's
already clinging to my legs, itching
like the bites on my arms, the whine
of another mosquito in here somewhere,

the air so close my mother's voice
comes right in — "OK, Frank, give me
one of those things; maybe the smoke'll
keep these bugs away!" — bringing my head
up to the window-sill, to her face
laughing in the match flare, tip
of the cigarette that lights my father's
face and Frank's and Helen's too
glints off glass and the metal
rim of lawn chairs. Even the lake
stops nudging the dock for a minute,
lets the night come in, as it can
maybe once, twice, in the whole summer,
when the dark fills up that hot, still air
with something close to clarity.

But what can I call that glimpse
I had then? Or explain why it shines
from my mother still, sets off
what I love in her? How the look
on my father's face (that look,
I see now, that happens when those we love
reveal, as they did the first time,
something we thought we'd lost
to the work of simply getting by)
burns through my memory, lights up
whatever I know of their marriage, of the weariness
and caring and surprise that brought me here
and from which I watch my own kid
take his bearings from some act of mine,
caught briefly, at a distance
further than that night seems now.

A night I offer you, those faces
cupped by darkness, lake and shoreline
as a hand cups a match for the moment
it is needed, even in a light wind,
unable to tell you more or why.

Caught, as I used to be,
by that trick an aunt or uncle'd use
of always stopping right at the best part
to take a bite of pie, a sip of tea,
their way of leaning back to look
around the table, let the story sink right in.
As if they hoped to find
that opening in each of us
from which, long after we'd been told
what happened next, they could begin
their slower, more miraculous
returns.

JOSEPH MACLEOD DAFFODILS

HOUSES

for Jim Rhodes

A woman looks up from her after-dinner coffee
to the garden where her husband leans
checking his broccoli, the curve of his bum
something she's still in love with
after all these years. Scarlet runner beans
climb the bamboo trellises he's built for them,
crazy trees, like the ones that rose
from his discovery that melons could grow
upright, each fruit supported by a muslin sling,
brassieres the neighbours called them,
but it worked, and the woman sees all this
(sees yellow marigold among the purple
stems of beet leaves, red nasturtiums
curling through the lettuce patch)
framed by a kind of generosity
she thought only painters had,
while a block away, in the upper half
of a stucco duplex, a young graduate student
has just met her new roommate's boyfriend,
a market analyst from Ottawa, whose sister,
it turns out, is married to a doctor, Peter
Mathewson, the same Peter Mathewson
the graduate student went to kindergarten with
in Thunder Bay, twenty years ago. "I can't
believe it," she keeps saying, as she pours
more wine, "I really can't believe it,"
though what choice does she have?
It's a small world and, besides, it's
the only life she'll get, a fact
that her neighbour, three doors up,
is also coming to, and hating
as he hates how his wife has to help him
out of the car and up the stairs, into bed.

"A minor operation," the doctor told him,
but that's not what the man feels now
as he curls around this new pain, this absence
of some part of himself he'd never even
thought about, ignorant as most of us are
of what really goes on in there.

Or maybe that's not it
at all. Maybe the woman glares
over her cup, hating the old fool, fussing
and fussing with his goddamn plants, the dead
white strip of skin between his shirt and
his trousers as he bends reminding her
of everything she can't love anymore
and he can't change, like the ache
she feels in her joints these nights
when the rain gets in and brags of its power there;
maybe Peter Mathewson married a stewardess, won
a lottery, moved to Monaco, maybe the boyfriend's
a sexist jerk who farts at the table.
The graduate student looks at her roommate
again. The couple up the street come home
with their new twins, his parents meet them
at the door with armloads of yellow roses,
the exact same yellow as the babies' blankets,
the lawn chairs in the yard next door, the shorts
on the young girl watching from across the street;
"I don't believe it," someone murmurs, as the door
swings shut, leaving the words alone, outside
the houses in which lights are turned on, drinks
spilled, letters started, baths run, where a man
calls out over the rush of water or his own thoughts
to whatever he thinks his wife just asked him
from the next room. "Of course," he hollers,
"of course I do!"

FAST CARS

for John & Lindy Stevenson

I liked how you arrived
for dinner last night, your arms
full of roots and cuttings for my garden,
how the music I was playing brought out
some crazy incident from your high-school days
so that soon we were all telling: first, those parts
we think we're old enough to laugh at now
and later, all that other stuff,
what Flannery O'Connor was getting at
when she said that "anybody who has survived his childhood
has enough information about life
to last him the rest of his days."
(How she should know,
her own life narrowed
to the distance she could cover
on crutches, on the farm
where her mother cared for her
and her stories grew, grace
like the brilliant turquoise of her peacocks,
widening before our eyes.)

I don't know how long
we sat that night. On the back porch
the plants leaned out through the dark
to the next day, the earth I'd turned
ready for them. But I know it was late
when we reached our own children,
all of them eager
to head off into whatever we fear
will take them furthest from us.
Booze or secrets. Sex. Fast cars.
How these things worry us, even as we know
that theirs may be the last generation

of kids on earth, our hearts contracting,
as they must, to what they think
they can comprehend.

After you'd left, I thought of a story
I hadn't told and how it fit with one I had:
when I was twelve, my best friend's brother Roger,
sixteen and drunk, went through the windshield
of his friend's Volkswagen two days before Christmas.
Six months later, the presents were still there,
unopened, on their hall shelf, and for years
my dad went on and on about German cars,
how dangerous they were,
another rant I had to tune out
with the rest of his war stories.
But if Freud's right about anything,
then it wasn't an accident
my first boyfriend drove one. Yellow.
That was the boy I told you about.
Doug, of the green eyes, who took me to a beach
that smelled of lemons for no reason at all,
the boy who taught me to drive the twisty road
to the highway, both of us pissed to the gills
all that summer when I got neither killed
nor pregnant and my father didn't know.
Didn't know as he glared from the doorway
every evening when Doug picked me up
and we drove off laughing.

And that's where we left him last night.

It's only remembering that other car, that
other child, that I can turn to find my father
smaller now, his thin shoulders rounded
as if to protect his chest and the knowledge
he has to keep there, as we all do,

for himself. Me, just driving into it then.
And him, just letting me go.

No. I should have said
having to.

THE WATERMELON INCIDENT

It was during this same summer,
in the back seat of another
speeding car, that I nearly
cut my finger off, slicing watermelon
with a jack-knife. We were all laughing
when the knife went in
to the bone, when it sucked out
one of those silences through which
blood spurted over my hand and onto the
watermelon, onto my other hand, my
knees, staining my new black and white
checked pedal-pushers which my mother said
were too tight anyway, made me look
cheap, like the peroxide streaks
Lorraine and I put in our hair when she
was babysitting at the Neilsons', onto
the grey plush seat and down to my
ankle socks, to my white sandals, onto
the floor, until Lorraine said "Jesus
H. Christ," and the car pulled over
rolled to a stop where we all got out
and stared. Two miles away,
the city bristled with hospitals,
antiseptic, doctors, cat-gut,
parents and tetanus shots, but we
were Beyond All That. Immortal.
And it's because I mean this
literally
that the bleeding stopped
that the end of my finger hung,
by a strand, from the rest of it
that Lorraine found some bandaids
she'd stuffed in her purse in case
her new shoes gave her blisters

that they held
that my mother was cooking dinner
when I got home
that my brother poked me in the ribs
and chewed with his mouth full
that nobody asked
that it was after the sun went down
(and in that sudden way a sunburn
will) that the pain surfaced.

Through my sleep, my hand
the size of a boxing glove
as if all the blood still in my body
pushed to that spot
where the bandaids held me together
and on whatever cool square
of sheet or pillow
I could find for it
kept it up: *pound-pound, pound-pound*
pound-pound, pound-pound,
until I knew for sure
it'd wake my parents
sleeping in the next room.

I'm one of those people
who believe that we remember
everything, though we may not know it.
Just the other day, in fact, I read
that even though we forget what we learn
when we're drunk, it'll all come back
sometime, when we're drunk again.
And that made me think
of the guy who lived in the apartment next
to the place I had before my son was born,
one of those buildings where so much
has passed from one room to another
that the walls thin out,
like those spots in an old shirt

where grease or sweat's been scrubbed at
so that the skin shines through,
so that every Friday night, when this guy
got drunk, I could hear the bottles
dropping, empty, to the table top
and by the tenth, maybe, the twelfth,
he'd be on to his mother, how he'd
disappointed her, he'd start wailing
and pounding the walls. Most of the time
I hated him, this old fart, sobbing
in his beer for Mama. I'd turn
the T V up or go for a walk,
but other nights, I guess, he must have
got in with my own sounds, somehow,
like those bits of dreams you never
quite let go, until this thing
I read on drunkenness and memory
opens the door for him and he sings there,
fiercely, in the midst of all the other stuff
about the watermelon and the knife
missing it, the blood and Lorraine's face,
the pain pounding out from my finger
to my wrist to my chest to my throat, my teeth
clenched over it, my parents
sleeping, soundly, on.

ONE OF THE THINGS I DID BACK THEN

Funny what returns and how you can't predict
what you'll use it for,
how the smell that means summer to me
isn't roses or freshly mown grass
but that hot-baked dusty steam
that rises from the pavement
just after the street cleaner's gone, gritty
and warm as any memory worth the work:
so a little girl stands
at the curb's edge in her bathing suit
catching the fine spray, the wave
from the driver.

How that memory leads me
to another. It's 1968 and I am standing
in the sweaty basement of the library, smelling
the must and mildew of old newspapers, the dust
coating my fingertips as I search
the birth announcements for 1948, '49,
checking them off against the deaths
and when I find one (*someone*, who died
in infancy) I write his name, the dates
on a card, and go on
to the next stack of papers.

Somewhere, someone else
who is 19 or 20
waits for this information.
Perhaps he is at my apartment sleeping
or drinking beer in my kitchen. Perhaps
he is walking nervously in the park or
riding a bus into town. Perhaps
he is still in the jungle, half a world
away, in Vietnam, trying to figure out

how to get here, though he doesn't know
where 'here' is yet. No matter.
When he deserts,
his real name becomes a skin
he has to shuck, so he can wear
the one I'll give him, a dead child's,
that allows him a birth certificate,
a social insurance number, a chance.

The rest comes in pieces.
All that stuff I saw later,
changed into movies — the young men
pushed from helicopters, the children
bursting into flames — I met then
for the first time, a war
coming at me, not from the T V
but through my own front door, born from hands
that dried dishes or made soup, carried
my groceries in from the car, from faces
belonging to guys who'd refused their deaths
as they'd tried to refuse the lives
they'd been doled out, always hoping
something better would turn up.

Mostly I see what I did back then
as a way I had to help them,
but sometimes I think about the parents
of the babies whose names I stole, how they'd feel
if they knew and whether it was a kind of violation.
I remember the excitement
of finding each one, like winning a lottery,
and how the names, the two dates
made the cards I used
look a little like tombstones,
those "letters of recommendation
to the dead," Berger has called them,
" . . . written in the hope that they,
who have left, will not need to be renamed."

Here, we know only too well
the chances a name offers
or denies. The difference it can make,
like the bit of luck or the casual decisions
that add up to a lifetime.

Here, I know, too, that the war
I thought I had a tiny part in stopping
merely shifted location and goes on
as planned.

And once, I remember,
I went back to June 2, 1945,
found my own birth,
announced with everything else,
proof of my own passing
into history, the future, my place
in the world and what
I would make of it.

GIFTS

Right now, my son is crying
because the T-shirt he bought me for my birthday
is a bit too small.
He has flung himself on his bed
and his sobs carry him out
and further away from me,
the sound of them sinking
into the noise of the party downstairs
like the stubborn intervals
that try to force a song apart.

As for the shirt, it's not that small
and I'd wear it anyway,
because of the Mickey Mouse decal
he's had put on and my name, too,
because he saved up for it
because I'm his mother
and he's my child, all that corny truth
that would have been enough
even a year ago
and isn't now.
He can see for himself how it wrinkles
under the armpits and clings
to my shoulder-blades.
He can see it's not my style,
just as he knows he can't exchange it.
Can't take it back   can't take it back;
it's the chill of that,
laying its damp yellow touch
on the fine brown arm of his love
for years to come,
like the words we let fly
in the midst of an argument,

how they natter, dry birds,
in some empty room of the brain.

It seems all summer I have watched
this growing in him, seen it rise,
unbidden as that gesture he has for impatience,
my own, made with his father's hands.
Seen it glistening like oil on his skin
as he measures himself for the world,
studying how the older boys
dive from the raft at the cottage
and then, alone, practising all morning
just as his dad might concentrate
on the tongue and groove of a shelf, the slide
of a desk drawer, a perfect fit.
But when the big boys
rocked the raft until it flipped,
a huge thing, coming down
in a crash of water, shouts
from the beach, I saw him
in the shallows with the younger kids,
small against that spinning instant
when you'd have to jump free
or get your head bashed in
(how you'd have to be sure
you could, sure
as you could be)
saw the grey pinch of his cheeks
as he entered this knowledge
the way he'd enter
any other element, that first breath
that took him from me
stinging his lungs,

or when, as now
he returns for a while
from wherever his crying took him,
grinning up at me in this crazy shirt,

the cost of it already pinned to his chest
an old badge, so that soon
we will return together to the party
which is for my birthday, the day
when we begin to learn all this,
taking a lifetime just to recognize ourselves
and one day
from that whole terrible journey
to celebrate it.

JOSEPH MACLEOD DAFFODILS

for Isabel Huggan

"I'm planting perennials this year," you tell me,
"because I'm scared and it's the only way I know
to tell myself I'm going to be here,
years from now, watching them come up."
Maybe it's a phase we're going through,
since I'm at it too; lily of the valley,
under the back hedge, thinking *when Jeremy*
is old enough to drive, I'll have to divide these,
put some under the cedars there; by the time
he leaves home, they'll be thick as grass,
and at the same time saying
"God, we're parodies of ourselves,
sixties children, still counting on flowers,
for chrissake, to get us through."
Knowing you'll see it that way too,
your snort of laughter
the index of my love and the wisdom
of George Eliot's observation that
"a difference of taste in jokes
is a great strain on the affections."
(Another thing we share, our delight
in quotations like that, exactly what you'd expect
from girls who grew up wearing glasses
into women who read everything;
your bathroom so much like mine,
a huge bin of books by the toilet
and on the shelves, all the bottles
turned label side out.
"The contents of somebody's bathroom,"
Diane Arbus said, "is like reading their biography.")

This doesn't help much, does it?
You're laughing, but your hands stay

clenched in your lap, still forcing
the tight, dumb bulbs into the ground
as if you could force your life
to a pattern as serene as theirs,
a calm that flourishes in darkness
to the pull of the sun.
Still, I keep on talking.
It's the only wisdom that I've got.
How about this one: you know those
big, yellow daffodils — they're called
Joseph MacLeods — well, the way they got their name
was that the man who developed them
always kept a radio on in the greenhouse
and the day the first one bloomed, in 1942,
was the day he got the news
of the Allied victory, against Rommel,
at El Alamein, and the announcer who read the news
was Joseph MacLeod. Which shows a sense of history
I can appreciate; no *El Alamein Glorias* or
Allied Victory Blooms for this guy, you can be sure.
It's like the story my mother always tells
about joining the crowds on V-E day, swollen with me,
but dancing all night, thinking *now*
she can be born any time.

What I love
is how these stories try to explain
the fit of things, though I can see
your mood's for something more sinister.
Like the reason Diane Arbus gave
for photographing freaks, maybe?
"Aristocrats," she called them,
"they've already passed their test in life."
Being born with their trauma, that is,
while the rest of us must sit around, dreading it.
Meaning you and me. *Normal.* Look at us,
practically wizened with worry, hunched
over coffee cups, whispering of cancer and divorce,

something happening to one of the kids, our lives
spread between us like those articles you read
about Mid-Life Crisis or Identity Anxiety,
Conflict of Role Expectations in Modern Marriages,
the kind that tell you you can fix all that
with less red meat and more exercise,
the ones that talk as if the future's
something you decide about,
though what it all comes down to, every time,
is making do. You can call it a choice
if you want, but that doesn't change
what we learn to rely on,
the smaller stratagems. Whatever works.
The socks in their neat balls, tucked on the right
side of the drawer, the iris coming up each summer
in the south bed. "Be sincere and don't fuss."
"Noble deeds and hot baths
are the best cures for depression."

It's what I love in you, Isabel.
How you can stand here saying
"Brave and kind. I want to get through this
being brave and kind," squaring your shoulders
like a heroine in those movies our mothers watched
where people knew their problems
didn't amount to a hill of beans
in this crazy world and let it go at that,
fitting themselves to the shape
a life makes for itself without meaning to.
I love your grin from the end of my sidewalk
as you head for home, posed like a photograph.
"Perfectly Ordinary Woman on Suburban Street."
"A secret about a secret," Arbus called this kind,
"the more it tells you,
the less you know."

TESTIMONIES

THE MAN WITH THE SINGLE MIRACLE

Here is a man whose life surrounds him
like a house outgrowing its owner.
Surrounds, but doesn't protect. This isn't
safety I'm describing, here
where the morning light gets in
on the sly, prowls around the edges,
sniffing out the dust
before it gathers enough of itself
to pounce. He never gets used to it.
There's always that moment when he can't remember,
when he imagines he's been brought here
drugged, at night, by strangers,
even his hands grown part of some mechanized nightmare,
tools he only operates, but doesn't understand
as they reach for his clothes, the smell and texture
what his body takes for reassurance.

Of course you know the sort of guy I mean,
with a job he likes enough to keep,
a wife he thinks of as his best friend
and kids who seem to be having
the sort of lives he'd hoped they would.
Like all of us, right, this man
whose jaw tightens in the sad part of a movie
though he knows it's really schmaltzy,
who believes they'll find a cure for cancer
before he gets it and assumes that his friends
are much like himself, wary of the way the days grow up
hodgepodge, like those places you find on the backroads
where no one bothers to plan anything.

This is why he is glad when they get together,
drinks and cigarettes, the stories they tell, he loves it
when someone just starts off slowly,

their voice as tentative as a kid's fingers
tracing line and squiggle on a page
till DOG or CAT leaps from the paper
in a sudden widening of the eyes.
He loves how his friends build their lives
into stories like that; even he has one
he tries to tell, though it never comes out right.
It's about the witch
who lived at the corner of his street
when he was eight and he always begins with her house
which you couldn't see for all the shrubs and trees
so he tries to explain how it felt, how the air thickened
and the sidewalks narrowed to a breath
you had to squeeze through on your way to the corner store.
At least he wants to make it that slow and heavy,
but his voice always sticks to his heart somehow
and the next thing he knows it's raced right on
to the part where he finds himself
in her kitchen, just staring at her
sitting there in her rocking chair
and how the thing he notices first
is that she is drinking milk
straight from the carton,
sort of pouring it down her throat
the way he does when his mother isn't around,
and he doesn't even know why this is so important,
but it is, so he tries to show them
how it goes with the smell of oilcloth and
onions — that was it — and how that smell fitted
the worn patch of linoleum under her chair,
a patch that warmed to the round, stinging
bite his dime made in his clenched fist.
Except that none of this comes out right
because before he's even finished
his friends start trying to figure out
how he got into the house in the first place;
but once they get going on dreams
or astral projection or some crazy theory

he never has a chance
to tell about being back on the street again
in front of the store, his ice cream
already oozing over his fingers;
or how just as he plunges into it, he raises his eyes
to where the road up ahead ripples and shines,
the whole city gone liquid, rushing
to the tip of his tongue.

You can see his problem, can't you?
And you can see how hard it would be,
getting together with his friends
on Saturdays for drinks and a couple of laughs.
Even the words he'd need, for one thing, belong
in the faces of those creatures
every city tolerates, their ramblings,
if they ever get you to listen,
nearer to prayers than anything else.
Besides, he loves his friends. Even this need
for explanations is something he feels tender about;
how can he help letting them rummage through his story,
the new owners of a place he can't keep up anymore.

This man I'm telling you about
lives in a city near a lake and by January
the harbour's usually frozen over
so that the people who live on the island, two miles out,
start driving to work instead of lining up for the ferry.
Pretty soon there's a good-sized road packed down
where someone in a truck has marked the treacherous spots
with oil drums or old Christmas trees,
though there's hardly a year goes by
that a car doesn't go through.
The city council tries to pass by-laws
forbidding cars on the lake, but by then
everyone's out there, so what can you do.
His kids love it, and every Sunday
they beg to go walking to the island.

Once in a while, he can feel the ice shift under him,
more like sound than motion, how it heaves up
from his feet to his throat, and though he knows
there's no real danger, what he trusts most
is that everyone else is out there too.

Only sometimes, this gets all mixed up, crazy,
like at a party when he'll feel that same
rise and swell pressing into his lungs,
when he looks over at his wife,
laughing in the corner there
or at someone else starting,
a little unsteadily,
towards the kitchen,
and he wants to call to them,
but he can't, any more than he can believe
what he sees; how their deaths
quicken the air around them, stipple their bodies
with a light like the green signals
trees send out before their leaves appear.
All right, he *won't* believe it then,
but doesn't it come to the same thing
for all of us? So frail, how could we bear
this much grace, when it glances
off the odds and ends we've no idea
what to do with, the jumble we just can't
throw out, stuffed into rooms
full of corners, old women
with cartons of milk at their lips
rocking back and forth.

FAMILIARS

That they should come back now,
to this part of my life
and not just through dreams either,
but sidling into daythoughts
with the same unerring timing that they mastered
was it fifteen, no, twenty years ago.
Those two. Zed and Zelda
I called them. For a joke,
though they came to fit their names
or maybe their names, like anyone else's,
came to mean what they were, how
can you tell?
Zed was just that — lean and abrupt,
determined too; I used to imagine her
chain-smoking and giving orders, like Joan Crawford
in *Mildred Pierce.* If there was anything wrong
with the food, Zed let me know, for both of them,
while Zelda sat around grooming herself
all day, always pretty and fluffy, outside
and in, a real airhead; she could have starred
in every beach party movie ever made.
I called her Zelda because I couldn't imagine her
without Zed there, and everyone thought
it was so cute, how she snuggled up to Zed
at night and licked her ears, while Zed kept
one paw around her shoulders, always.
Cute, we all said, how they loved each other
like the kittens on a calendar,
like those cartoon shows
where cats and mice and rabbits
are really humans in disguise

as if the thought of their being anything else
were far too lonely for us to bear.

When Zelda died, Zed found the body.
And after that, she sat in their box
with her face to the wall, howling;
I want to say crying, but that's
wrong too, just as my trying to tell you
how she went skittish and grey, crazy-eyed
like someone on speed, won't explain it either
and anyway, she left about then
so that I only saw her in the alleys
or around the garbage by the pizza place,
though once, a year later, she came back
limping and, well, hardened somehow,
to sit in her old spot for a while
looking out this time, at me
from a distance wider than any
a common language could have filled.

And she's back again. I can feel it,
just as I think I see some of her look
in the one I'm getting
from my own son these days, the one
he brings out during the argument
we're always having, the argument
neither of us can ever win
(and which winning wouldn't matter anyway)
the one that began with his first word
and slowly clarifies itself, like a photograph
in a developing tray, what my son holds up
as evidence: the life he sees
out there, away, in the future.
At 13, he carries
the little I've had time to give him
easily, just as I hope he'll lose,
someday, the weight of my failings
which are heavy now, like the scorn

he bears me. *I love you* I say to him
I love you, almost afraid,
like when I was a kid and believed
you could only use a word so many times
before it flickered out, a flashlight
with a dead battery.

So, lots of times I talk to him
inside my head, though I don't like to.
It's too much like the conversations
I catch myself having
with a friend who's died, when I want to say
you and mean it, unable to believe
I can't anymore, just as I can't imagine
her body, sunk through death
until the earth's become the only air
it takes in and releases, more slowly,
more surely, year after year.
This is the power she'll have for me
always. As my son will.
It's why the cats are back. Those two,
Zed and Zelda, and then just Zed,
that crazy grey cat out there, past
the reach of our comfort, our human
laughter, that other animal
come back, in broad day, to sit
in this room with me and stare
from across it all.

43

BENEDICTION

for Peter D.

The unexpected rituals that grow
out of an ordinary life, like those acts
which by their constant repetition
fix themselves in the cells, the muscles
folding more than we remember
into their layers of tension and release,
just as the objects we possess
may tell the stories of our lives
more accurately than we ourselves could.

A wedding ring and the art
of making pastry are all I have
from our marriage, Peter.
The one's almost too small for my finger now,
but the other's a rite by which I am returned
each time I perform it
to that first, crazy summer,
all the wasted flour and tears
cursing cookbooks and rolling pins
until (like making bread, like
riding a bicycle) it arrived
to live in my fingertips, my brain,
so that each pie I make
recalls that first perfect one
set down before you, recalls
the young bride and the year
that cut so deeply into my life
it found its way to my palmline, the mark
each fortune teller notices, right off,
before everything else,
that means I can't explain you
easily, the way I want to, with

some dumb cliché about children
playing house.

And that makes this news of your death
come too hard, damn it.
A voice I don't know on the telephone
says *cancer* says *peacefully*
and you're gone. Like that.
As if they'd taken my favourite photograph
— the one in the churchyard after the wedding
where I'm leaning against you, laughing —
and pulled you out of it,
so that I pitch backwards
wildly, my face convulsed
like a fool's or a drunkard's.

To imagine how I came
to this. My name on a list
you've made, probably, its writing
a time-travel as you moved through it
into that wider space
the dying need for their work.

I say "the dying" and mean you,
Peter. Each death specific
as the terms that bind me to it,
so that yours, which looses
the cells of your body, scatters
the details of our marriage too, the bits
that matter to no one else
I'd meant to gather in some day,
the address of our place on King Street,
and that couple downstairs
— the people we went to Mexico with —
her name was Helen, what was his?
                                    I miss you
more now. So young then, I thought forever
came with words, the hateful things

we never took back, not knowing
some people could and go on somehow
as if nothing had happened. How I said
I never wanted to see you again
and believed it, the way I believed
in childhood as a simple time
I'd passed through, dreaming,
into what I imagined
was a life of my own.

So I keep coming back to that list,
how my name must have brought you
into our life again, unseen,
already a ghost. Though who knows
how we reach each other, what ceremonies
will appease, when something so commonplace
as easy as pie will have to do for us. Will serve
as the touch to the tightened muscle
that loosens anger or grief, my voice
sent out to you at last
with its small song of forgiveness.

And how that too will be returned,
always, now, to me
who can still use it.

TESTIMONIES

for Julie Cruickshank

As the cadence in an old woman's voice
becomes the line that will lead others
into the territory her people saw,
you make me see
the importance of your work, the long hours
taping these languages which only a few
of the elders speak now. "My stories are my wealth,"
one woman tells you, "all I have to give
my children," and you help create the alphabet
that takes them there. Linguistic anthropology,
the science of making language
into maps. The crazy detours
it can take you on, that story
of the parrot up in Carcross, N . W . T . ,
a bird someone brought over the pass
during the gold-rush and left at the Caribou Hotel
where it lived for another sixty years
entertaining customers by singing
nineteenth-century bar-room ballads
in a cockney accent. The voice of a dead miner
kept on in a brain the size of an acorn,
all the countries of his lifetime, contracted
to its bright, improbable presence
amid men who figure they've seen
just about everything now,
so that their sitting there, listening like that
becomes part of the story too,
just as I am added when I tell it,
as anyone will be, each version
a journey that carries us all along,
as the shards of pottery, carefully labelled
and carried up through layered villages

flesh out more hands
than the two that made them.

How can any of us know
what will speak for us or who
will be heard? We who are never
satisfied, eager for the evidence
no matter how it comes, slowing the car down
as we pass the accident, to see
what's pulled from the wreckage, crowding
the ones who were at the scene, the cop
or the ambulance driver, the survivors
stepping forward for their moment, blessed
by our terrible need to know everything.
Even those women we dread
sitting next to on buses or trains,
their bodies swelling with messy secrets,
the odour of complaint on their breath,
may be prophets. Whether we listen or not
won't stop them from telling
our story in their own.

Not far from where I live, a man ploughs
someone's skull up in his cornfield
and the next spring, four more, a family maybe
though no one knows even that,
their being there at all,
and longer, the only claim that's offered.
Like the farms themselves, their few rich fields
the chance deposits of a glacier.
Even the ones that I keep looking for,
wading through goldenrod to a house
where just inside the door, the trunk of old clothes
or the chair that didn't make it
to the load on back of the truck
bears witness to those smaller choices
we all have to make

about the future
and what can be wisely carried into it.

What your work brings you to, I see now,
not the past. Each site, a threshold
into this slow discovery,
the random testimony gathered
as best we can, each of us down
to essentials, as the failed are
and the dead, who bear us forward
in their fine, accurate arms.

FOOD

for Marty, and in memory of Jessie Glaberman

Begin where we all do
with milk. How I still like mine
straight from the cow, driving out
to a farm each week, through fields
dotted with Holsteins, the only landscape
I can understand. My dad says the stuff
that's really worth drinking's
squirted warm and straight from the teat
and I believe him, just as I know
his city life's the instrument
that pries that memory loose
from the history he hated, the narrow
caked path from pasture to barn
and the blistered sun at his neck
day after day. Just as I know
for me, too, it's more nostalgia
in the glass, as even the smallest farms
become factories, the cows hooked up
from udder to tank to truck
to pasteurization plant
and on (in just a few years, probably)
to what's become of beef or chicken, things
kept in buildings never opened to the sun.

Food. Or the politics of food. You see
I did learn what you tried to teach me, you two:
your house on Bewick Avenue, your table
where a union man from Bologna might meet up
with a woman from a feminist commune
in New Mexico or a kid from Oregon, on the road
for the summer, who'd heard about your place,
everybody hashing out their differences
over meals that went on for as long

as our appetites lasted and the wine held,
Jessie at her end, pushing her glasses up
with one hand, passing food with the other,
Marty at his, finger out, making some
theoretical point someone else had overlooked,
living up to the joke we made of his habit,
as soon as he'd open his mouth, we'd laugh
and call out, "and then Lenin said . . . "
loving him for it.

Just as I love you, Marty,
for that whole hot summer
when you taught me to read *Capital*
of all things, as I thought no book
could be read, cold theory warmed
by those hands of yours, the lines
that oil and grit had eaten there
part of what you were saying, just as the smell
that clings to hair and clothes gives off
the heat of a factory, the noise,
fights with foremen, meetings, wildcats,
always at it, "The working class
is revolutionary or it is nothing" — Karl Marx.
"But not a slogan," I can hear you saying,
"a statement of fact; either we'll manage
to change things or we'll disappear,"
your finger out as you say this, the other hand
reaching for chicken or coffee, refusing
to separate food from what it costs.

Jessie, in the only snapshot I have
your mouth's open, of course, your face
blurred by what you were saying at the moment,
words freed as carelessly as the smoke
from your cigarettes, filling the air
and disappearing. At your end of the table
everything was always up for grabs;
"Spit it out," you'd cry, when we fumbled

for a straighter phrase, "don't be afraid
to say what isn't finished, what seems
crazy. Just say what you can;
we'll look at it together."
And we would. All of us,
peering into those dimmer, tangled
regions theory doesn't open on
and though I bet we'd argue still
about what got said those nights,
we'd all be hearing your voice
angry, laughing, leading us into them.
Oh, Jessie, it drives me crazy
knowing you died alone,
how you must have hated, struggled
and in another movement,
taken it, knowing we are always
alone in this, your shrug
— I can see it still — what I have
of you, your work
that widening of the wild zone
between the power to fight what happens to us
and the power to accept what is.

It's late afternoon in the old house on Bewick.
In the kitchen, someone's poking around
trying to decide what to have for dinner,
while in his new apartment
Marty follows an argument about Poland
from the stove, where he's making
his famous stir-fry, a recipe
I'll use myself tonight, with tomatoes
and zucchini from my garden, snow peas
from the guy in the third stall, second row
at the market, soy and ginger, Basmati rice
from I don't know where, and while we eat
I'll tell my family how I heard
on the radio today the future's
in kiwi fruit, a new type, hairless

and the size of grapefruit, more vitamin C
than a dozen oranges and easier to ship.
I'll tell them how scientists
have developed an apple tree
shaped like a telephone pole, no branches,
fruit straight from the stem, for easier
picking and bigger profits and while we
take this in, women I've eaten with
are adding sour cream and red wine
to their pot roasts, as Jessie
taught them to. For all I know,
they're quoting Lenin and Marx,
maybe the FBI is right, subversion
is everywhere.
Oh, I know, I know, it's late
in the century, the revolution hasn't come,
the hungry go on, food costs the earth,
the work of getting enough
breaks us all, I know, I know,
but even so, the tomatoes
are red, ready to sting
my tongue, the smell of their vines
clings to my arms, Marty talks
with his mouth full, his finger
urgent as always, a woman throws
a handful of parsley in the pot, a taste
brings me up to her, and it's that
I'm telling for the moment, just
for now.

ANNIVERSARY

in memoriam, Pat Logan

The road turns off
just where it always does and rising
comes out to the second corner
where the graveyard is.
Your grave. You. Behind us,
in one of those reforestation stands
the government plants, the pines
grow taller in their narrow columns
as if to show me how there can be order
in returning what we owe.
I remember what someone told me
of a woman whose husband took her ashes,
as she'd asked him to, and with their children
travelled for a year to scatter them
all over the world, a gesture
that tries to say what death allows
in each of us, no matter how we meet it.

It makes me want
to tell you everything:
what I ate for breakfast,
my son's French teacher's name,
how my basil's doing this year
or the deal I got on this Lincoln rocker
from an antique place I've just discovered
on the Wilmer Road. The man there — you'd like
him, Pat — who told me how he'd farmed
for years and years and then risked everything
on something else he loved,
his hands stroking a desk or chair
just as they've bumped the right curve
of a cow's belly, learning the season
of the calf within, listening to wood now,

what to bring forth
from layers of decisions made by strangers,
for their own good reasons.

Remember that day you taught me
how to look for four-leaf clovers?
"Don't try so hard," you kept saying,
"just peek from the corner of your eye,
like this," running your fingers
through a patch and coming up with one
every time, surprised as I was
and with no more faith, but opening
your hand out anyway, that gesture
which belongs to any gamble,
no matter how crazy, the movement
by which a life gets changed
for keeps, a reach
for what we only hope
is there

just as this yearly journey reaches
deeper into what I only thought
I understood: your death
is final, and touching that
brings out the colours — certain
as the grain in oak or cherry —
of a wider life that grows
through the small demands the present makes
pushing me back to the car for the ride home,
already planning the sandwich I'll get
at the truck stop on the highway; empty now,
the woman who runs it taking the time
to put her feet up, sink back
into the knowledge that will hold her
until I arrive; my wave, her smile
what we'll begin with, the common
courtesies, as if they were nothing
to be surprised by.

BONES

INTERVALS

I. Entry

Enough people tell you how comfortable it is
and you come to believe it,
this city opening up
like the map it hands out to tourists,
the parks and the reasonably priced restaurants
enclosed in circles, innocent and reassuring
as the arrows leading you back out to the 401,
the songs on the radio tracing
the same old terrain, love's body
where the prince and the princess live
happily ever after.
Your own childhood. A small girl
eating her spinach out of duty
to the starving, those ragged figures
who still lurk at the edges of polite conversation
like the cities they inhabit, the televised names,
the pictures where women walk through markets
full of soldiers, and kids play
near a parked car, where anything
can happen any minute; though when it does
there's always someone there
between you and the damage, a voice
over the shots of bodies, letting you look
up from the screen
to the square of street outside,
and back to the weather
which will be fine, tomorrow rising
as it always has, with those
who are never asked.

All that talk, what was it
but a need for safety, your life
running on automatic
for as long as you let it,

right up to that night (exactly like any other,
you think now, exactly) when a neighbour
knocked on your door, some figure
from a backyard painting of blue arms,
white squares on a clothesline
suddenly there, a woman, coming to you
her face full of blood, the night
spilling out from her hair
to the street, the man, light glinting
off the metal in his hand
as you pulled her inside.

Where that night's taken you since.
This city, an edge like any other;
its dark, the border territory between houses
where violence holes up in men's hands, the shadows
that fall between a woman's breasts, the kids born
already knowing. Like time bombs, all those childhoods
huddled in corners, these houses
wired to the world, the hum you hear
when you pass, the TV's blue light
spreading into the street and inside
the people, frozen by it,
just sitting there,
waiting.

II. Free Speech

This is for Sylvia
who is deaf
and whose teeth are rotted to the gumline,
stumps in the foul swamp of her mouth
where the noises she makes at us
only her children can understand.
The oldest, fourteen, is smaller
than an eight year old, his wrists
thin as the pencil he's using

60

to mark off the days
their father left them alone, locked
in their cabin forty miles north of here.
Ten, maybe — the pencil hesitates —
no, twelve, with a bag of flour
and a box of powdered milk,
before the cops broke the door down.
This is for him too, for Steven,
round-shouldered old man of a kid,
one hand on the paper, the other
in the air, signing to his mother
the little he has to comfort her
in any language.

Interval House.

Interval: originally
from the Latin inter vallum,
the space between ramparts,
walls, between two events,
two parts of an action, a period
of cessation, a pause

This is for Ruth,
brought in by the police
from Hotel Dieu emergency
eyes swollen shut, broken jaw wired
and eighteen stitches closing one ear. This
is what a man might do
if his wife talked during the 6 o'clock news.
"And I knew better," she tells us softly,
"I guess I just forgot myself."
Tomorrow she may go back to him
("He didn't mean it, he's a good man
really"), but tonight she sits up with me
drinking coffee through a straw.
"I can't sleep," she apologizes,

"every time I close my eyes,
I see his fist coming at me
through the wall."

A house that can accommodate
20 according to regulations,
30 in a pinch, since we don't
turn anyone away, 32
if we use the old couch
in the back office, maybe 35
if most of them are children
which they are

For Marilyn, aged 7,
her arm crushed because she caught it
in a wringer washer, where she was left,
alone like that, for three days.

Between any fits or periods of disease
an open space lying
between two things
or two periods of one thing

This is for all the time
it's taken me to learn
that terror is not always
sudden, as I thought it was,
the fist or the bomb
ripping the sky open;
that often it is slow
and duller
as August stupefies a city,
that glazed season we come to
out of helplessness,
the wound shut off
from the eye, from the brain

going on, going on alone
behind sheets and sheets of anaesthetic.

The distance between persons
in respect of position, beliefs, etc.
or between things in respect of their qualities,
the difference of pitch between two
musical sounds, an opening

a gap

a 24-hour crisis line

this is for the voices
on the other end I never see,
for all they have time to tell me
before something stops them.

III.   E C U: On the Job

If I were to place my hand on the side
of her head, the bruise at her left temple
would exactly fit the palm, the heel
curving over her left eye, where the rim
of the heel of her husband's shoe has left
a gash marked out by the doctor's stitches,
which I follow now
applying this ointment to the dry, stretched
and healing skin, beneath which there is only
a thin plate of bone between them
and her brain, where everything happens at once:
the sting of my touch and the ringing of the telephone,
someone laughing in the kitchen
where the dishes are being done, the work
of her lungs as they empty
and fill themselves, the noise
her children are making upstairs

and what will happen to them now;
the brain is adding hydro to food
to first and last month's rent, phone bills
and cough medicine, trying to make ends meet
while it keeps the heart
pumping the blood to her wound,
food for the new cells,
pushing her slowly into the future,
the bruise already yellowing at its edges,
though her husband's still there,
flung into her life again,
nothing left between them but the days
exactly alike, each one bought
at the same cost, and that too
the brain is trying to calculate, a numbness
deep in its centre somewhere
which keeps her eyes turned from mine;
so that for now, her bruise
is the only currency between us.
I carry it home like a paycheque,
my fingers smelling of ointment and blood,
and when someone asks me how it went today
it is the bruise that spills from my mouth,
uncontrolled, incurable, it stains my son's cheek
and grows in secret on my breasts and thighs,
shoots from my husband's knuckles
as he sits there, quietly peeling an orange,
becomes the dark between us in the bed at night.

And maybe it can't be helped.
Maybe it's only what any job
on this planet makes of us,
the shoulders rounded over fifty years
at a sewing machine or a desk, the lungs webbed
with black dust, the cells of a foetus
altered by an eight-hour shift at a computer terminal
day after day. How we've made it seem normal,
when I open the door at 3 a.m.

and the cops are there with another one,
three kids in pyjamas, a few clothes
in a green garbage bag, how this
is just part of their night's work,
as the blood on her cheekbone there
is mine, our daily bread bought with it,
all that we're capable of
and all we can be made to endure,
until even the smallest of us, the babies
I see each day, flinch
when I try to pick them up;
so that that gesture, that grotesque
twisting from another's touch
embodies a future
which includes us all, exactly
as the child growing in the salty fluid of the uterus
includes everything our cells remember
of the long swim in from the sea.

Our future. Though it may be no more
than the last few years of this century
already so full of horrors
that perhaps it can't be helped,
this bruise, no bigger
than the palm of my hand
and beneath it, a woman's brain
still urging her forward.

Something as small as that.
The time we have left
to see it.

IV.   Short Story

This isn't one to be told
in the third person,
though we keep on trying to.

65

My friend describes what happens
with the couple upstairs in her building
and it's like an old movie, only
just the soundtrack, no picture
of the man whose footsteps fill the hallway
outside her bedroom, fade
to a muffled clumping on the stairs
and return with a bang
when the door comes open
over her bed.
Then the thin, unsteady rise
of a woman's anger, and a man's
trying to make her
keep it down. What happens next
could come from westerns or The Three Stooges,
all the slaps and punches, sharp
and exaggerated, the high-pitched clatter
of chairs, but when it falls
from her own ceiling
it's as if she's never heard it before
like the softer thud that blossoms, finally,
in the darkness nearest to her face.
Like any of us, she's frightened
by what she doesn't know
and she tries to explain it
somehow. By the bottles that come out
with their garbage every week
or the dirty children
clogging the front porch.
"Or maybe that's how those people
want to live," she tells me,
as if they choose a life
like a slice of bread, cut clean
from the loaf and eaten with honey
in a warm kitchen.

As if.

So a four-year-old stands in a doorway
yelling at his mother. "Cunt," he screams,
"cunt face! Nothin' but a fuckin' cunt face!"
his words, like the life he's been given, a genetic code
forcing him forward, a blunt weapon,
forcing the story on that way
(this story about *them*, about *those people*)
so that we who hear it can forget
how little is ever really possible
for any of us, botched
failed things to whom it may only come once
and never clearly, that moment
when the voice that tries to sing
through all our stories rises, briefly,
first person singular,
cries *yes* and *now* and *help*
help me.

V.   Departure

Always the same beginning:
words and the cells that make them
all that will carry us
into the future.

"I want to get in touch with my feelings,"
a friend says, as if they lived elsewhere,
as if there were more than this, our real selves
different from what we make of each other,
what we accept: these houses
where language capitulates and love
is something to be beaten
out of another's body
or in. *Am I getting through?*
we say to whoever we think
is in there, inside the body
which isn't it,

is a dirty word, allowing everything
that's done, violence taken in
like oxygen becomes the skin
we wear, the atmosphere the planet
turns through, its orbit shrunk
to the will of those
for whom our bodies
are obstacles and nothing more.

In Argentina, a group of scientists
sifts through the mass graves
the death squads planted
cataloguing scattered bones and teeth.
In five months, they make ten
'positive identifications' as they call them.
Ten names. Their eye sockets and jawbones,
their knuckles filled in, their bodies
making room for themselves
out of the numbers this century rushes through,
white noise.

We are that close.

Each of us, who are only
the work of our lungs as they empty
and fill themselves,
the back, the arms
the cells' need, the brain
where all this happens all the time.
All of it and only that.

We are that close.
The time we have left
to do it.

NEIGHBOURS

for Lorna Crozier, who asked

Though don't think you're the only one.
Everybody does.

"So you're from Kingston. The prison town. Well,
what's it like down there, with all those
criminals?"

Sometimes I tell them
Clifford Olson is my next-door neighbour,
he and the other rapists and baby-killers,
their lives down to a few square feet,
a narrow hour in the exercise yard
a block from here at Kingston Pen.

Sometimes I describe
the time I went to P4 W
to teach a writing class
where the first woman I met
with her red hair in rollers, a red flowered
housecoat on and those slippers with the pom-poms
also red, red toenails and fingernails,
looked like everybody's aunt from the Big City
who is always more interesting than your mother,
though the truth is she'd chopped her husband up
with an axe.

Another way to answer your question
is to talk about the geology, history
and architecture of this city, built on rock
and out of it; about whether limestone
just naturally piles itself into forts

and prisons, churches, universities, mansions
for the rich or whether the people who settled
couldn't see anything else in it
but their need to wall something in
or out. I could introduce you
to the man whose backyard touches mine.
A retired guard, he'll tell you
things are worse than ever, prisons
run like luxury hotels by asshole politicians,
con-lovers, like the lawyers and social workers
who've never seen the ranges where the guards work;
how can they know? Somebody knifes you
and they act like it's your fault
for being a screw in the first place.
He stuck it out for the pay and the pension,
this house, university for his kids. Not bad
for a guy who never finished high school,
though now he's got this lung disease
and the doctor says it doesn't look good.
Stooped on the back porch, grey and wheezing,
he coughs up forty years of smoke and anger.

A while ago, someone
broke into a friend's house
and beat her unconscious.
For no reason. She came up
from a deep sleep and he was already
there, his hands at her throat.
The police were amazed
when she came to. They showed her
pictures and pictures of young white males.
Is this him?   Is this him?
More amazing, she refused to testify,
though all she'll say is that she doesn't feel
prisons are the answer. Her face, when she speaks,
is calm, repaired now, though I think I can see

ragged places in the darks of her eyes
that he tore there, for good.

Some days, when the cries of other victims
rise from the headlines,
I think what she says
is the biggest pile of crap
I've ever had to listen to.
Others, I hear in it
the sound that flows through those who've come back
from a few hours' dying, a current that runs
beneath their descriptions of white light
and someone there to guide you into it,
a parent or a friend, someone from before.

This is when I remember
how the layers of limestone match
the fluctuations of an ancient ocean,
just as the fields outside the city
ride the wider movements
of the rocks that formed the continent.
I remember how the streets here
follow the meeting of lake and river
so that you never end up
where you think you're going to.

Some days, when the guy at the back
comes out to say hello, his look
is the one my dad's face had
after his heart attack, that big man
suddenly lying there, staring up at us
for the first time, embarrassed to suffer
what so many others have already had to.
In his grey face, something opens,
softly. Like those colours

that tint the skin of limestone
when you really look at it.

Some days, I drive home
through fields July's brought little to
but the common yellows of hawkweed, mustard;
colours, I read somewhere, that insects see
as ultraviolet, a luminescent landscape
we can't use, though the city
rises from it, scared and hopeful,
like a friend I haven't seen in years
who wants to show me in her walk
or how she's done her hair
another way of wearing
everything I thought I'd recognize.

CHANGE OF HEART

"Ford Madox Ford taught that you couldn't have a man appear long enough to sell a newspaper in a story unless you put him there with enough detail to make the reader see him."
— Flannery O'Connor in "Writing Short Stories"

It was my aunt who taught me
how to pick the last tomatoes
when they were still green
and wrap them in newspaper,
store them away in the dark
where they'd ripen on their own,
surprising me with their colour
long after the red was gone
from the trees, the dried leaves banked
around the sage and the oregano.

I still don't know how they did it,
there, without the sun.
Or why I want
to let them surface here
when I'm trying to write
about a change of heart,
as if some homely metaphor
about it growing sweeter,
like a piece of fruit,
is going to make it easier
to tell you
it belongs to the man in the last poem,
the man you saw long enough
for him to beat my friend unconscious.
You're no Pollyanna. You know
the real thing, the warning
your own heart gives out
when you're alone, at night, crossing

the parking lot to your car, knowing
the guy's still out there.
It's me who needs to put him
here, describe the night it hit home:
this was it, his one and only life,
the days that followed, documented evidence
of a changing heart, maybe some A A meetings
or an upgrading course at the high school,
the job he's held for three years now,
his wife and their new baby.
I'd like to make it
his voice, coming to you
as the one witness you can trust,
but instead, there's only mine.

I have a friend with fair hair
and a way with children.
One night a man broke
into her house and beat her up.
She survived and after the bruises
finished with her, she got up
and went back to work. As she does
every day now, waking every morning
to that silence which surrounds
her life, in which she must decide
again, and for today only,
how she will live with the memory
of his fists. And I tell you
my need to believe this
is the closest I will ever come
to faith, that atmosphere
in which no one I know
can live, very long, any more.
Me, here, trying to survive it
long enough to make you see
how my friend, who decides
each morning, also remembers
as I believe the man who beat her

remembers her screams, and each day
has to make from them
a way of speaking to the muscles
that control his hands, to the stammer
he thinks of as his changed heart,
and to the finer chemistries
that make up, and renew him,
every seven years, exactly
as he is, affirming everything.

BURN-OUT

is what happens
when you work too hard
in one of the *caring professions*
as they're called these days.
It has definite symptoms
and most workplaces now
offer seminars to discuss it,
distribute burn-out pamphlets
in the staff room.

For me, though,
it's my old apartment on West Street,
after the fireman turned to where
I was standing on the sidewalk
and said "OK, we'll take you in now
for a minute." How the place was
colder than I'd thought possible,
the broken windows, the walls
smeared with soot and the wet
grit under my feet. And the smell,
the smell I couldn't get out
of even the few things
I wanted to try to save.

Beyond that, it's the door
to the staff office at Interval House,
a shelter for battered women and children.
I'm sitting in there now,
the walls around me plastered
with kids' drawings, notices, telephone messages
and photographs, at a desk littered with coffee mugs
and matchbooks, ashtrays, a telephone
and the book you record the calls in, a soother,
pens, a bottle of shampoo, some cough drops,

a kid's mitten and two pairs of earrings. It is
8:30 p.m. and I am only
four hours in
to a twelve-hour shift.

I wish I could tell you
that the kids are all in bed,
the women getting ready
to watch a movie on TV,
someone making popcorn in the kitchen.
I wish I could lay in a music track,
as I could if this were a film,
so that you'd catch snatches
of Holly Near, maybe, or Joni Mitchell,
yes, even my tinny, six-year-old voice
way back there in Sunday School, singing
Jesus bids us shine with a clear,
pure light because, damn it, that's
here too, but not tonight.

Tonight,
I have eight more hours to go
when Linda comes in, shuts
the door, lights a cigarette.
Her face has that look
I've learned to recognize
but tonight, all I know
is that it's just my luck
to have to be here, watching
as her mouth forces the words
out from some hidden place
so far within her she might
never have found them, never,
into this room, where they become
a job I'm not quite
up to, not tonight " . . . it wasn't
alive, I mean, but it was
something, you know, I was maybe

five months along, and afterwards
he got a kitchen knife to cut the,
you know, the cord and put
it in a garbage bag, he
wouldn't let me go to the
hospital and that was a year ago,
I never told anybody, but
I have to
now."

And again, I wish I could tell you
how I handled this in a
professional manner, except that
I, personally, don't think there
is one. Professional always makes me think
of when I was at school
and the teacher told us
there was no such word
as the word "can't."
"You *can* do it! You *can*,"
my gym teacher screams at me
as I gather for a broad jump, leap
into some weakness in the joint
a grandmother'd left me. For good.
An accident it's called,
that juncture between
what happens to you
and what you have
to meet it with,
which isn't always enough.

So Linda and I
just sit here. She's crying,
but for a minute more, I still hear
the doctor, standing over me
shaking his head, talking of
" . . . *chondromalacia* . . . *osteoarthritis* . . .
due to repeated injury, which

always burns itself out, so that
the joints, though stiff of course,
are ultimately painless,"
and I reach
for my knee (cradling it
as I might a child's head
sleeping, in my lap) as I will
in the next movement, reach
for Linda's shoulder
in that gesture which,
from where you are, may appear
ambiguous, whether it's for
comfort or support, though
believe me, it's not
the distance makes it
seem that way, it's not
the distance, at all.

BONES

for Barb

A story of yours got this one going,
so I'm sending it back now, changed of course,
just as each person I love
is a relocation, where I take up
a different place in the world.

The way you told it, it was after midnight,
you coming off the late shift, heading home
in a taxi, a woman driving,
and you ask her if she's ever scared
working these hours and she says, "No, I've got this
to protect me!" reaching under her seat
to pull up (you expected a crowbar,
a tire iron) this eight-inch, stainless steel
shank. "The pin from my mother's thigh,"
she tells you, "I got it when they put
one of those new plastic ones in."

Sometimes when I tell myself this story
I get caught up in logistics,
how the doctor must have delivered the thing
from layers of fat and muscle
into one of those shiny dishes
the nurse is always holding
and then she would have,
what? washed it off? wrapped it in towels?
carried it down to the waiting room, the daughter
sitting there, reading magazines, smoking cigarettes?
It's so improbable, like the foetus
pickled in a jar in the science lab in high school,
though other times it's just
there, natural as the light
that bounces off it,

somebody's mother's thigh bone,
for protection, like her face
in the hall light, rescuing you
from a nightmare.

You told me this
during my visit last year
when I'd just quit working
at the crisis centre, that job
that wrenched me round
until each morning stretched, a pale, dry skin,
over the real colour of the day,
ready to spring at me, like the child
whose hand had been held down
on a red-hot burner
reappearing in the face of a woman
met casually at a cocktail party.
Everywhere I went, my work experience
drew me through confessions I couldn't stop,
and I couldn't stop talking about them
so you had to listen
but, being you, in that way that listening
can be active, when the listener re-enters
the country of her own damage
from a new direction.

This can be like watching someone we love
return from the limits a body can be taken to
— a botched suicide, say, or an accident.
Years, it might be, before the eyes or the hands retrieve enough
to offer as a sign,
what doctors think they can detect
on a CAT scan, some pattern in the cells
to show them, once and for all,
how the mind, like the body, makes shape
of what's left, the terrible knowledge

it labours through, slowly regaining itself.

Though on an x-ray, even the bones show up
as light, a translucence that belies their strength
or renders it immeasurable,
like the distances we count on them to carry us,
right to the end of our lives and back again,
and again.

NEARER TO PRAYERS THAN STORIES

KOKO

"Hands developed with terrible labor by apes
Hang from the sleeves of evangelists. . . . "

— Robert Bly in "The Great Society"

Only now it is our terrible labour
(or what we thought was ours, alone)
unfurling from the root-black fingers
of an ape. Koko, the talking gorilla.
In Ameslan, her hands are muscular
and vibrant as vocal cords, name
colours and distinguish *had* and *will,*
can make a metaphor; they choose
a tailless kitten for a pet
and christen him *All-Ball,* lie
when they need to and insult their trainer
Penny dirty toilet devil, a repertoire
of over 500 words that upset
Descartes, Marx, our known,
human world. Not to mention fellow linguists
who say it's all a trick — Polly, Polly
pretty bird or Mr. Ed. They point
to her IQ score, a meagre 85,
though when they asked if she'd choose
a tree or a house for shelter
from the rain, she chose a tree
and got marked wrong.

Who says
and what
is what it comes to, though,
the sky filling up with satellites,
the cities with paper, whole stores
of greeting cards for everything
we can't spit out ourselves,

like the scratch at the back of the brain
we no longer recognize as memory.

On the TV Reagan and Gorbachev in Geneva,
though their names don't matter much,
just two more faces over shirts and ties
discussing missile size, the "nitty-gritty"
as a spokesman puts it, while
"women are more interested in peace
and things of that nature . . .
the human interest stuff."

The human interest.
Kinda like the swings in the park
across from here, how they always
squeak, day in, day out.
The guys who trim the grass
and keep the benches painted
don't even try to fix them anymore;
they know some things are like that,
stubborn as hell, no matter how much
you make an hour or what kind of government
you get. So that what we have are humans
in Oslo, Leningrad, Peking, Thunder Bay,
Denver, Cordoba and Rome pushing their kids
on swings that *squeak   squeak   squeak*
like the creaks
and farts and stutterings the body makes
to say *here* and *here* and *here.*

After living with them,
Jane Goodall found that chimpanzees
use tools, which leaves us language
as the last thing
we've got, we think,

and at the compound, Koko looking out,
a reporter tries to keep it:

"Are you an animal or a person?"

The hands coming up, almost
before he's done: *Fine animal gorilla.*
Close to the chest, showing him
familiar palm and fingers
sing *fine* caress *animal.*

SEEING IS BELIEVING

for Kathie

You tell me you believe in magic
and at first I'm with you, fitting
your words to my own vision: how hard work's
made these paws of ours subtle enough
to pull a rabbit from a hat
or rescue Venus from a hunk of rock.
But then I see you mean it
literally, that look in your eye
the warning light at which my mind
brakes and switches to reverse
like the flashing orange note I can hear
at any distance when someone starts up
about intense religious experiences;
" . . . they talk of hallowed things, aloud,
and embarrass my dog," said Emily Dickinson
and I agree, stiffened in my chair
while you trace, with thin
quick hands and endless cigarettes,
a fourth, fifth, eighth dimension
from which birds and wolves
appear at will, worlds
we can travel to ourselves,
"as we used to," you say, "by flying
outside our bodies!"

Outside your windows,
your prairie winter stretches
further than I can, Kathie,
my imagination bumbling
like a fly awakened in the wrong season
against these tiny squares
that open onto so much sky.

And from the tapedeck, a song of Ferron's
fills the space this side with her
brand of longing — *I am looking for something*
outside of forgiveness — the last notes
following the smoke from your cigarette
into the light you're silhouetted by, the white
of the next field stunning my eyes
as they find someone else out there
moving alone and steadily into it.

I want to cry out to them
"Be careful! Be careful!" but I know
it's me I'm really talking to.
Just like the other day
when we were driving into Calgary,
all that white, that sky again,
and I wanted to ask you, "Kathie,
are you here for good?"
as if I could make your choice
a question still, after fifteen years.
I remember the road coming
to a slight rise then; there was this
white house, a barn and a few
scraggly trees that you slowed for,
"Look," you said, "I love that place,
it's so much like Ontario," laughing
at my shriek of denial, but sticking
to what you'd said, both of us right,
just as a woman can see
why her friends can't understand
what she sees in some guy
and go on seeing it
at the same time.

So, Kathie, you've brought me to this notion
that the place we end up in
goes deeper than choice, if we're lucky.

Do you know what I mean? How a friend
in Toronto suffers from allergies
that clear up
the day she moves to the west coast,
while some one else writes
to his family in St. John's
from Australia, saying "I'm home at last!"
I never was to Africa, Ferron's singing,
but it comes up in my dreams
and though we'll never be able to chart it, probably,
it's in our blood, what geneticists will come to
in a lab someday, some ancestor's love
for a climate or a skyline
reaching out to plant us
in the place where we'll do best.

I'd even call it scientific,
though I know you'd hate
the word, want to soften
the borderlines between my brand
of magic and your own: all those countries
where we range, halfway between hope and theory.
Just as I imagine you some days,
driving, driving, your need
mapped by wind and that sky
always moving, always reaching
to that point on the horizon
where limitation and possibility
seem to come to the same thing,
while I write this in Ontario,
February, that month when grey and white
is all I see, but see it
as I hear the sound that grows
in Eastern prayer chants,
African drumming, from the way
a single note is played
a little differently each time, until the music

fills these fields, whose movement
to the time it takes
to wear a mountain down
sets even the oldest landmark drifting.

NIGHTWORK

"Every day is thought upon and calculated, but the night is not premeditated."

— Matthew O'Connor, in Djuna Barnes' *Nightwood*

I always wanted to be the one
who drove the snowplough, me
and a tall red thermos, like the one
my dad took into the plant, high up
in the cab, driving through it. Could see
the sun, rising on the arc
the wipers made, like the waves
from the neighbours, sleepy and bundled,
digging their cars out as I passed.
And then it was flour
I wanted to plough through, mounds of it
falling around me in a bakery,
the round loaves rising;
and after that, the white uniforms
of nurses, cool as their hands
pulling someone up from a fever dream,
from the middle of the night.

Later, of course, I read Marx
and learned that bakers in the 1860s
died in their thirties, exhausted
from their eighteen-hour shifts, children crushed
in the rolling mills where they'd fallen
asleep, after twelve hours. Later,
I learned for myself, that year
in the parts plant, how the days
fall in on themselves, as they did
when my son was small,
when my grey need for sleep

drifted like cobwebs
through my brain cells.

And yet, even then, I remember
standing by the window, his hot
damp cheek on my shoulder, looking out
over the city to the lights of the supermarket
where someone was piling the shelves
high with cans of peaches, opening some
to share at coffee break
with the guys from the meat department
who'd grilled a couple of steaks,
maybe fried some onions and mushrooms,
one of the ways they'd found
to cut the losses the job left
in the only time they had, like the calls
that office cleaners make to relatives
in England or India, "all over the world,"
one of them told me once, "a whole life
we build up for ourselves, from the big
fat desks of I B M executives."

And I remember the night I was in labour
with my son, when the doctor arrived
in a tuxedo, looking worried. It was
his anniversary and they'd just sat down
in a fancy restaurant, to champagne,
when his pager beeped. "Get me out of here
by nine," he laughed, "and I'll buy you
a bottle of Mumm's." I did my best,
though it was hard to imagine him
with another life outside of
this one; "Open your eyes,"
Ron whispered, as I hunched,
pushing, and I saw my son's
opening into mine
as his head emerged
as his shoulders slid forward

as he was lifted to my stomach
where he turned toward me, as any
animal will, smelling sex or food.
Later he took my breast, that first tug
travelling to my fingertips, the narrowest
pocket of my lungs, each fold of brain
or intestine, every crease
in the soles of my feet,
like light coming on
in a room I'd only half-inhabited
to show me for the first time
exactly where I was, how I belonged
to the laughter of the nurses
as they changed shift, and to that
of the doctor and his wife, dancing,
Fred and Ginger, among waiters, musicians,
chandeliers, women with jewels in their hair,
Ron's kiss, as he left, the snow
just starting in the streets outside, the tracks
of his tires from the hospital parking lot
to the one at Harvey's, cheeseburger and shake
handed out to him by someone pimply and heavy-eyed,
the skid into our driveway, last night's paper
stuck in the door, the telephone operator
awake, ready to place his call, bringing
my mother to the news she'd waited for, for years,
my mother, standing in the kitchen, calling
Air Canada, VIA, my father putting
the coffee on, the man who drives
the snowplough, starting up.

THINGS

My first car was a blue Volkswagen beetle
Mike Longmoore built for me
out of the old parts that sprouted in his backyard
overnight, like mushrooms;
and something that car took in
(maybe from the rain or the cryptic soil)
gave it an organic personality.
I'm not saying it was anything like a human,
or even another animal we'd recognize,
just that it was a car you didn't *drive,* really.
Instead you had to think of *going places together,*
and only those who understood this perfectly
could get it to start in the first place.
Of course, I talked to it; clumsily at first
just as you learn to converse with your dog
or your maidenhair fern, but gradually
I got the hang of it, though I wasn't there
the day my brother took it to the beer store
and the big green Pontiac with the drunken salesman
came through the stop sign; so I can only imagine
that moment, between impact and shudder,
when it realized it was only metal after all.

Of course, that car's not the only thing.
A pair of green shorts I had
when I was fourteen, the exact shade
and texture of summer. Or a salad bowl
I've seasoned so often, we wear each other's smell
as lovers do, another kind of skin.
A rag doll my brother brought me
from an Indian woman in the mountains of the Yucatan,
herself in miniature, wearing her clothes,
her eyes and nose stitched in with yarn,
and below that, where the mouth should be,

a blank she'd left
to tell of the silences between women.

What is it for you? The thing you love
for the beauty of it, heft
of a well-turned bowl or the singing precision
of a sharp knife, how the foot feels
against the spade that slides willingly
into the earth, tables that make
the mouth water, chairs without spiritual pretensions
who know that their duty is to the body
in all its moods, the carved walnut box
for keeping secrets in,
all the hockey sticks, axe handles,
canoe paddles, tennis rackets, boomerangs
that come to you
from those who use wood
to tell what they know of movement,
all the things we make
to nourish the body and its life,
whatever takes its purpose
from our limitations
and seeks to bless them
even in small ways.
That is our history here
though we had to get out of the trees to make it.
Before that, everything we share
with the chimpanzees, hanging around
picking nits off each other.

Now it's things that connect us.
They are social beings after all,
leading complex, cosmopolitan lives.
The woman who cuts my hair has these scissors
she spent hundreds on. They're worth
every penny too because they
understand so perfectly
whatever her fingers tell them

even though she has to send them to Japan
once a year to be sharpened.
"Because only the person who made them
can do it properly," she tells me,
"it's the way things are." She's right, of course,
and there are hundreds of scissors like hers
all over the world. I can hear the clatter
their stiletto blades make in the airports,
their round eyes cutting through clouds
as the plane descends into Tokyo.
And as for the plane, what is it
but a thing we've made to carry
other things? And ourselves, too, but only
to buy and sell things, find out
how other people make them, trade them,
take pictures of them, staring at the ones
that live in museums and art galleries,
scrounging the earth for those still
caught in it, left behind by the dead,
their lives frozen in them
as blown glass holds the glass-maker's breath.

Once the Neanderthals had tools
they dug graves where archaeologists
can find the dust of flowers
someone placed beside the body.
For a purpose, which still
reaches out, palpable,
ambiguous as a word
or the hundreds of gestures we've made
to say *yes* or *no*.
That coffee mug you hold each morning
without even thinking about it
is a mystery. Reveals what our need makes
from sand and heat, what it trusts
to cardboard boxes, straw, metal staples,
asphalt, diesel fuel and the oily roar
of jet planes. Is a lifetime

on the road or in a factory,
the fifteen-minute break the guy
who loaded the plane is taking
at the edge of the runway before he loads
the socket wrenches for a bike shop in Utah,
a Coke in one hand, a cigarette
stinging his lips. A greeting,
borrowed from the earth to bring comfort,
holds us.

STUNTS

(a poem inspired by The Guinness Book of World Records *and an interview with Philippe Petit in* People *magazine)*

The ones they can't pull off
bring us nothing. Houdini's dying promise
to return. How he must have climbed into his death
with the simple faith he'd demonstrated
all his life: if there's a way in,
there's a way out. Counting on us
to believe it this time too, forgetting
the fist in his gut, the abrupt fall
into what it made of him.

Forgetting his body like that, though the trick's
there or nowhere, doing it over and over again
until it comes, another way of talking.
What the high-wire artist means
when he says that running is the acrobat's laughter.
"When my heart is open to the wind," he tells us,
"I am next to the gates of Paradise. Our domain
is bounded by death, not props."
And we can see how he holds to that,
the balance pole that gives him
the patience of one who has fallen before
and believes he will get
what he deserves.

As we all want to.
So that when Annie Edson Taylor,
first person down Niagara Falls in a barrel,
climbed out and said, "Nobody ought ever
to do that again," nobody listened.
It wasn't her advice
that got her over, any more than it's the air
that keeps the divers from the rocks

at La Quebrada or the roar of the cannon
that Zacchini flies with, at 54 m.p.h.
When the wind cuts through our overcoats
as we walk home from work, we know
Petit feels it too
as he steps out between the towers
of the World Trade Center,
1350 feet above our heads;
and as our fingers fumble for our keys
we are glad for the ones
that keep a yo-yo going, 5 days
non-stop, or write the Lord's Prayer
34 times on a postage stamp.
We know what they look like,
no further escaped from a fin or a claw
than our own; so that it pleases us,
when the day boils up
smelling of burnt milk, when we're out of coffee
and the egg runs down our chins,
to know that someone's out there, for us,
making omelettes while dangling from a helicopter,
catching a grape in their mouth at 319 feet
or climbing a 30-foot coconut tree
in 4.88 seconds, barefoot.
To know we're deserving sometimes,
as Petit steps out
into that instant, bounded by air
at the edge of the crowd's hope,
where everything comes easy
and the body fits.

ORDINARY MOVING

From here, I see my son round the corner
on his skateboard, heading home,
knees slightly bent to steer the thing
around parked cars, a wiry dance
in which the body pivots
on the bump of the wheels, while the feet
stay firmly grounded, save for one last move
— after he's turned it up the driveway to a spot
just there — when he jumps off, flips it
with his toe to lean against the back step, ready
for take off, the whole performance
that mixture of nonchalance and theatre
I recognize from the movies, especially the ones
where Bogart shoves a handful of hundreds into his pocket,
uncrumples them later for drinks or the cost
of straightening a girl's club foot, his way
of tipping his hat or lighting a cigarette
filling the screen with his past,
with the present state of the world, even
as clearly as my son fills out
his thirteen summers in a curve
that brings the littler kids
up from their sandboxes, just to watch.

Sometimes a voice can do this too.
That auctioneer I heard last week,
one of the best, I'm told, though my
poor imitation — *in at eighty-five, who'll say*
ninety. I've got eighty-five, who'll say
ninety. Ninety's in, who'll give me ninety-five,
ninety-five, who's got ninety-five.
Ninety's going, do I hear ninety-five.
Five. Five. Do I hear ninety-five. Sold for
ninety dollars, number one-eight-six — can't give you

her hands, singing their part, threading
the air between the high, gold line
of a Gibbard sideboard and the grey eyes
of the woman in green, holding out for it.
You'll have to call that up
from yourself; the day, the yard
and what's in it, the house emptied,
saying *now what*   *now what* will all be
yours, just as the childhood
that returns when I chant *Ordinary, moving,*
Laughing, talking can belong to no one else,
though it's right where my voice
enters your brain
that our two childhoods meet.

On the beach, all the people
move through the heat between sand
and sky. Ordinary moving, all this
clumsy flesh, the gawkiness that mumbles
through its cramped litany of pain, getting
on with it, the scars half-hidden under
towels or T-shirts keeping their boasts,
bargains struck against a future
that must wait, a few years more,
to lay its claim. All the people move,
each body wearing more life
than it thought possible at first,
and worn by it too, proof positive
that nothing is ever past. Look,
that man there swings his daughter
to his shoulders, his hands so big
they cover her knees and hold her
up as surely as she and she alone
holds him. In the width of her palm,
or the length of her toes, in whatever
she takes from this hour, from its heat
and the smell of his skin rising through it,

from the sound of his voice,
for later when it's no longer his.

All these people, moving
on this beach of mine. Or yours,
like the auctioneer or the child
on the skateboard in whatever street,
whatever city, even Bogart grinning down
from a million screens, larger than life
and still no bigger than our own, each one
unfolding into another's, almost as easily
as parents come to love their children, those perfect
strangers to whom we surrender everything,
and as abruptly as summer arrives
in my part of the country — for a few
short weeks at best, but as if it were
the only season, ever, all its heat
spilling open
in a single afternoon.

IDYLL

The baby is playing
with an empty potato chip bag.
Or rather, *the* potato chip bag, the one
that dropped from her sister's hand
when she jumped up and ran
back to the other kids
splashing out there, where the sun
hurts her eyes. "Bag," she said,
"play with the bag, Kelly,"
and now the baby knows the crack
and glitter, the metal-salt
vinegar smell, the gritty
taste of the word, a sound
she can grow for hours in
like *milk* or *sleep.*

Behind her, the dog is chewing
on an old bone he's dragged
from under the hedge, his eyes
flicking from the baby to the beach
and back, up to the adults
sitting on lawn chairs, eating hotdogs,
sharing with them this love
of being in the sun, chewing
and watching other animals
(just as, in a recent interview,
a famous film-maker said
he got his ideas from shopping centres,
walking around with his walkman on,
eating ice-cream and staring).

For almost an hour the eight-year-old's
been trying to stand upright
on the inner tube, if only for a minute,

so that by now she knows
the stretch and tighten of calf and thigh,
the tremor her toes cling to
at one foot up, the slithering dip
of half-crouch to the sleek
whoosh slip beneath both feet
that tips her into a splat of cold.
Above her, she can feel
the sky's patience, gentle
as her mother's is sometimes,
letting her know she can grow
to meet it, just as her brother
on the dock finds how
to draw his afternoon around him
with the flick and curve of wrist and forearm
as he casts and casts
the bright rapala spinning to plop
near a stump or a rock, wanting only
that answering tug, sunfish or rock bass
he doesn't care, though he knows the story
of the big one down there, older,
his grandfather says, than the cottage,
feels it nibble at the base of his brain
while another part of his mind
swims back and forth,
trying to decide about noise
whether the younger kids
splashing behind him
bring the fish or scare them,
how some people say
you have to keep perfectly still,
yet Charlie Saunders catches more
than anyone, banging his frying pans
over the side of the boat
before he casts, "to get 'em
mad," he says and the boy plans
to try it, though he also knows
that "getting a fish mad" is an

anthropomorphism, the word his dad gave him
surfacing with a smile as he brings the rapala in,
looks at it, decides to try worms.

And all the time, the adults
keep on talking. Nothing stops them.
Though a question has to loop
and swim around a sand castle,
someone wading out too far, a toddler
reaching for a cracker, skinned elbows
and the need for more beer,
it makes its way at last
to bring the answer back.
Everyone laughs and the day
remembers itself, drifts on.
Someone starts to think about
taking the chicken out of the fridge,
maybe shelling some peas, when dark
against the far shore, a girl teeters
yelling "Mommy, Daddy!" a fish
flashes to the dock in a spray of light,
the dog jumps up, barking, someone
swings the baby to a hip, yelling
"Look at that!" and the crumpled bag skims
over the grass, eddies in the shade there
where the sun's hit the beech trees.

LIFELINES

"Like no one before
He let out a roar
And I just had to tag along
Each night I went to bed
With the sound in my head
And the dream was a song."
         — from John Fogerty's "Big Train (From Memphis)"

Now I'm no singer, so I used to think
I'd only come to music from the back door,
the sidelines, like I came to baseball
or motorcycles, always the passenger,
which was fine in its way, how Elvis
got me started, loud
as he could go on my green portable,
my father downstairs yelling
SHUT THAT DAMN THING OFF
ignored, as he had to be.
Like the night Elvis was on Ed Sullivan
— if only from the waist up —
and my mother's hands went
to her mouth, confirming
what I knew
about what I needed.

How I could ride
flat out like that, one voice
for a mood or a season,
years of Dylan when everyone I knew
or ever would know
seemed to be on the road
angry and sure of our destination
even if it meant just not going back.
Songs that opened into rooms,

the place I lived with Peter, "All You Need
Is Love" and "Brown-Eyed Girl," like the smoke
and the red wine that carried us
into the long, long nights; I could go on,
but you've got your own lifeline, surely,
humming it now, I'll bet, as you hear this,
confident that it will all come back,
"Teen-Angel" on the car-radio the other day
and me singing along, word-perfect,
everyone else suddenly silent
as if I'd just dropped in
from another planet.

Which I had, in a way,
all the brain cells
where I've stored the energy
for just that kind of travelling,
so that now I do thirty years,
easy, in an hour and not just
straight through, either,
detours and double-backs, leaps,
butting the Beatles up against the Talking Heads
or a voice like Ferron's charting
all the places Dylan's never will.

Re-mapping my life, you could say, the way
this poem began, with a song
and something smaller too: one of those styrofoam cups
you get for take-out coffee, Chris and me stopping
for some the other day, and him standing by the car
tearing a little hole in the plastic lid — you know
how you do, so it won't spill — and saying
that every time he does that
he goes right back
to all those dumb jobs, all those summers
on the rail gang or the paving crew, the years
in the paint factory, all the breaks
when he'd stand in the doorway

or the shade of the spreader, just staring,
the cup going cold in his hand.
The shock of it now, feeling
his heart make room again
for the wanting and wanting that cramped it
into the tightest corner of his chest,
that spark in a synapse somewhere
regaining for him
something else he thought he'd given up on,
saying *look, you have time, even yet*
to come to love this too.

My son asks if he's growing
every second and I say yes
knowing he'll go straight on
to bamboo shoots, while I catch
this crazy image of the double helix
spiralling at the centre of each cell,
my layman's view of D N A, bright filaments
of light or sound the body moves to
in the dance it makes through what it's given
what it's trying to become,

just as I dance on a Saturday afternoon
in an empty house, for hours sometimes,
all the selves I am ambiguous
and incomplete, as always,
as the same old rhythms rise
and change and relocate themselves,
keeping it up, keeping on
for as long as I do.

PARTICULARS

To come back, again,
to those Sundays at my grandmother's table,
but by a different way, so that I see
that thin spot in my father's hair
as he bowed his head to ask
the blessing — what my grandmother
called it, not thanks — *Bless*
this food to our use
and us to Thy service,
in Christ's name,
Amen. My father stumbling
over the words, perhaps in recognition
of what he was really asking for
(there, in the midst of things,
his whole family listening),
a blessing, on food they'd earned
casting metal, teaching other people's kids
or planted, themselves, in the fields we'd see
as soon as we raised our heads, men and women
embarrassed by prayer, but sticking to it
as they stuck to their stories,
hoarded those private, irreducible histories
that no one else would get a piece of, ever.

To begin to see, a little,
what they taught me
of themselves, their place
among the living and the dead,
thanksgiving and the practical
particulars of grace, and to accept it,
slowly, almost grudgingly,
to come downstairs this morning
as the paper slaps
the front porch, look up, catch

the paper girl with her walkman on
dancing down the street, red tights,
jean jacket, blonde hair, making me
love her, perfectly, for ten seconds,
long enough to call out
all my other loves, locate each one
precisely, as I could this house
on a city map or the day I found
my son, swimming within me.

To try and hear it
in the way we make the most
of what we get, like the man I know
who says he's held Death in his arms.
That's how he puts it, trying
for a way to say *wife* or *Ellen*
and reach far enough to touch her
there, include the whispers
from the hall outside, the hiss
of the oxygen tank, still on,
the sounds his arms made
adjusting to her weight, this
angle of bone, this one
when her head tipped, finally, back.

And to say for myself, just once,
without embarrassment, *bless,*
thrown out as to some lightness
that I actually believe in,
surprised (as I believe
they were) to find it
here, where it seems impossible
that one life even matters, though
like them, I'll argue
the stubborn argument of the particular,
right now, in the midst of things, *this*
and *this.*

A NOTE ON THE TEXT

Some of these poems first appeared in *event, Descant, Fireweed, Poetry Canada Review, Quarry, The Malahat Review,* and *Poetry Toronto.*

I want to thank Donna Bennett, my editor, especially for pushing me as hard as she did; Isabel Huggan, Jane Knox, Lisa Markon and Carolyn Smart for guidance and support; and all the women at Kingston Interval House for continuing to teach me how much it is possible to change.

Also, thanks to the Ontario Arts Council and the Canada Council for the money and time to work on these poems.

•

Note to "Intervals: ECU: On the Job" — ECU, or Extreme Close Up, is a cinematographer's term.